EYEWITNESS
DISASTER
TSUNAMIS!

HELEN DWYER

Marshall Cavendish
Benchmark
New York

Other Marshall Cavendish Offices:
Marshall Cavendish International (Asia) Private Limited, 1 New Industrial Road, Singapore 536196 • Marshall Cavendish International (Thailand) Co Ltd. 253 Asoke, 12th Flr, Sukhumvit 21 Road, Klongtoey Nua, Wattana, Bangkok 10110, Thailand • Marshall Cavendish (Malaysia) Sdn Bhd, Times Subang, Lot 46, Subang Hi-Tech Industrial Park, Batu Tiga, 40000 Shah Alam, Selangor Darul Ehsan, Malaysia

Marshall Cavendish is a trademark of Times Publishing Limited

Planned and produced by Discovery Books Ltd., 2 College Street, Ludlow, Shropshire, SY8 1AN www.discoverybooks.net
Managing editor: Rachel Tisdale
Editor: Helen Dwyer
Designer: sprout.uk.com Limited
Illustrator: Stefan Chabluk
Picture researcher: Tom Humphrey

Photo acknowledgments: Corbis: 19 (Bettmann), 20 (Lloyd Cluff), 21 (Supri/Reuters), 24 (Hugh Gentry/Reuters), 27 (Pallava Bagla). Getty Images: cover & 4 (John Russell/AFP), 5 (Torsten Blackwood), 6 (AFP), 11 (William West), 12 (Torsten Blackwood), 15 (Jimin Lai/AFP), 17 (Marco Garcia), 22 (Torsten Blackwood), 23 (Torsten Blackwood), 26 (Junko Kimura), 29 (Raveendran/AFP). Shutterstock: 10, 28 (Karin Hildebrand Lau). UNESCO: 25 (Commander Mily B Christman, NOAA Corps) US Navy: 13 (Mass Communication Specialist Second Class Andrew Meyers), 14 (Photographer's Mate 1st Class Jon Gesch).
Cover Picture: Residents and tourists flee as a tsunami wave comes crashing ashore at Koh Raya, Thailand.

Library of Congress Cataloging-in-Publication Data

Dwyer, Helen.
 Tsunamis / by Helen Dwyer.
   p. cm. -- (Eyewitness disaster)
 Includes bibliographical references and index.
 ISBN 978-1-60870-005-9
 1. Tsunamis--Juvenile literature. I. Title.
 GC221.5.D89 2011
 551.46'37--dc22
                            2010001801

Printed in China

CONTENTS

Words in **bold** or <u>underlined</u> are defined in the Glossary on page 30.

WHAT IS A TSUNAMI?

A tsunami is a series of ocean waves that are created when water in the ocean is suddenly disturbed. These waves can occur several hours apart. They travel unnoticed across the ocean but then grow to enormous heights as they approach a coast. In the past, tsunamis were sometimes called "tidal waves." This is not accurate since they have nothing to do with tides. The word *tsunami* is Japanese and means "harbor wave."

Displaced Water

A tsunami is usually triggered by an undersea **earthquake** that moves rocks in the seafloor. These earth movements **displace** the water above. The more the seafloor moves, the larger the tsunami. Other events such as **landslides** that fall into the sea, or even **meteorites**, will displace water and can cause tsunamis.

> " To me it was like a monster—just black water coming to you. It wasn't a wave that breaks, it was a full force of water coming straight."
>
> Luana Tavale, tsunami eyewitness in American Samoa, September 2009.

The first of a series of tsunami waves races over a beach in Thailand in December 2004. This massive tsunami struck without warning and devastated coasts all around the Indian Ocean.

Deadly Waves

Tsunamis can be several yards high when they finally reach the shore, so they can cause massive amounts of damage. They sweep away people and cars, uproot trees, and destroy buildings. Tsunamis often strike without warning. They are among the world's deadliest natural disasters.

Police in Samoa search a village well for victims of the tsunami that struck these Pacific islands in September 2009.

POISONOUS SALT

Apart from their ability to destroy and kill, tsunamis also leave behind other, long-lasting problems. Seawater contains salt, which in large quantities is poisonous to animals and plants. When salt enters soil, crops are poisoned and are unable to grow. Salt also seeps down into underground water supplies. A massive tsunami in the Indian Ocean in 2004 affected thousands of wells that provided drinking water in coastal areas. Many wells were destroyed and the water in others was made unfit to drink.

WHAT HAPPENS IN A TSUNAMI?

When an earthquake under the sea changes the level and shape of the seafloor, water is disturbed and waves form on the sea surface above the quake.

Wave Heights and Lengths

Every tsunami has different wave heights and lengths, depending on how the seafloor has moved. Scientists think that the size of the movement affects the height of the waves. The wavelength is the distance from the crest (top) of one wave to the crest of the next—often hundreds of miles. Far out to sea, these crests may be less than 3 feet (1 meter) high, which makes tsunamis difficult to detect.

Sometimes the first sign of an approaching tsunami is the sea being sucked away, exposing areas that are usually underwater. If people are unaware of this danger they may walk out to sea, like these people did in Thailand in 2004.

"I said, 'Pop, there's no water in the cove. It's all rocks.' . . . Then when we saw the water coming, everybody started to run, because it . . . was like it was coming from the sky. That's how high the wave was."

Mary McKenna, eyewitness to the Newfoundland, Canada, tsunami in 1929.

Speed and Depth

The speed of a tsunami depends on the depth of the water. In the open ocean tsunamis travel at about 435 miles per hour (700 kilometers per hour). As they approach land where the water is shallower, tsunami waves slow down and their wavelength shortens. As a result, the waves become much higher. Sometimes they take several minutes to reach their maximum height. The power of the waves as they hit the land is devastating. Some tsunamis can cause floods hundreds of yards inland.

AMAZING ESCAPE

Knowledge Saves Lives

In 1999 on the Pacific Ocean island of Fatu Hiva, French Polynesia, a school teacher glanced out of a window at the nearby beach. To her horror she saw that the water was draining away from the beach. Fortunately she knew this was a tsunami warning sign. She told the children to climb out of the windows at the back of the school and head for higher ground. Minutes later a tsunami destroyed the empty building.

Tsunami waves get significantly higher as they near coasts, when they slow down as the ocean floor under them rises. The water that flows over the land is called the run-up.

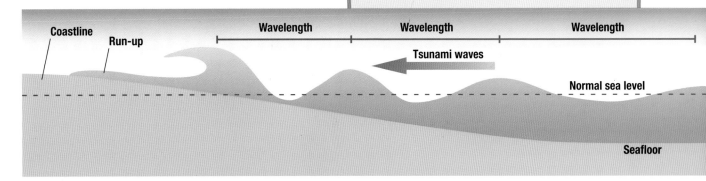

WHERE DO TSUNAMIS OCCUR?

Undersea earthquakes usually take place along the boundaries of **tectonic plates**. These plates are large sections of Earth's solid upper layer—its **crust** and the top part of the **mantle** that lies below the crust.

Moving Plates

Tectonic plates move around very slowly in different directions on top of the hotter, more liquid parts of the mantle. Sometimes plate edges become stuck to each other for a time, and then suddenly break free. This jerking movement creates ripples through the rocks—an earthquake.

Many tectonic plates collide near the coasts of countries in or around the Indian and Pacific oceans. These are the world's major tsunami zones. Another active tectonic plate boundary stretches through the Mediterranean Sea into the Atlantic Ocean.

Atlantic Tsunami, 1755

In 1755 an earthquake and tsunami in the Atlantic Ocean hit the city of Lisbon in

These are the world's major tectonic plates. As some of them pull apart, others collide, creating earthquakes.

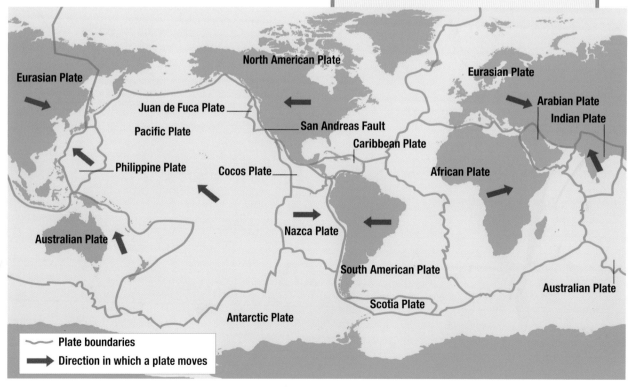

North American Plate

Eurasian Plate

Eurasian Plate

Arabian Plate

Indian Plate

Juan de Fuca Plate

Pacific Plate

San Andreas Fault

Caribbean Plate

Philippine Plate

Cocos Plate

African Plate

Australian Plate

Nazca Plate

South American Plate

Australian Plate

Scotia Plate

Antarctic Plate

Plate boundaries
Direction in which a plate moves

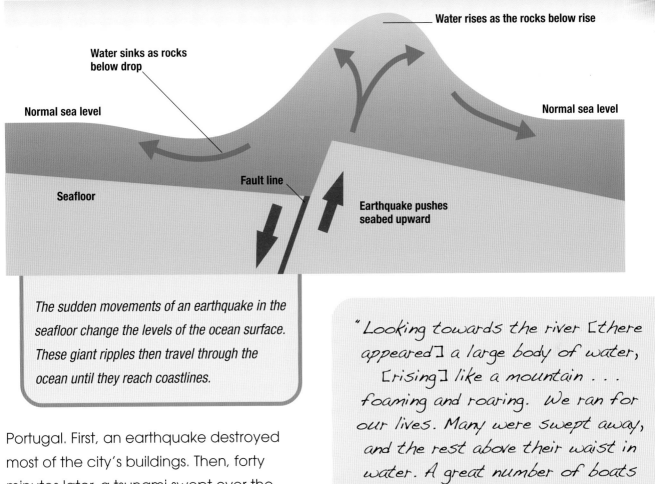

Water rises as the rocks below rise

Water sinks as rocks below drop

Normal sea level

Normal sea level

Fault line

Seafloor

Earthquake pushes seabed upward

The sudden movements of an earthquake in the seafloor change the levels of the ocean surface. These giant ripples then travel through the ocean until they reach coastlines.

Portugal. First, an earthquake destroyed most of the city's buildings. Then, forty minutes later, a tsunami swept over the harbor and city center and up the River Tagus. Four hours after the quake, the tsunami—then 10 feet (3 meters) high—reached the coasts of Cornwall, England and Galway, Ireland.

"Looking towards the river [there appeared] a large body of water, [rising] like a mountain . . . foaming and roaring. We ran for our lives. Many were swept away, and the rest above their waist in water. A great number of boats [were] all swallowed up, as in a whirlpool, and nevermore appeared."

Charles Davy, survivor of the Lisbon tsunami, 1755.

TSUNAMI OR TIDAL WAVE?

The 1755 tsunami in Cornwall was one of only two ever recorded in Britain. A few scientists, however, think that a destructive flood along the Bristol Channel in 1607 may also have been a tsunami. Writers of the time claim that 20,000 people drowned. Many church walls still have marks showing the height of the flood waters. Although a tsunami is a real possibility, most experts believe that the flood was the result of extremely high tides and storm winds.

HOW OFTEN DO TSUNAMIS OCCUR?

Disastrous tsunamis are quite rare. Small-scale tsunamis that cause minor damage are very frequent. Some tsunamis hit uninhabited coasts, so they often go unnoticed.

Deadly Tsunamis

In an average year, only one tsunami occurs that is powerful enough to kill people. In the twentieth century, there were seven tsunamis that each caused more than a thousand deaths. Some tsunamis hit largely uninhabited coastlines, causing few casualties. However, if a tsunami strikes a large city, thousands of people may be killed or injured.

> "The whole earth was made to shake and shudder, and the sea was driven away. . . . Many-shaped varieties of sea-creatures were seen stuck in the slime. . . . Then the roaring sea . . . dashed itself violently on the mainland and flattened innumerable buildings. . . . Huge ships . . . were hurled [2 miles] from the shore."

The earliest written description of a tsunami by Roman historian Ammianus Marcellinus in the city of Alexandria, Egypt, 365 BCE.

The region of Aceh in Indonesia was devastated by the Indian Ocean tsunami in 2004. More than 200,000 people died and half a million lost their homes in this part of the country.

An earthquake in the Solomon Islands in 2007 raised some areas by 10 feet (3 m), exposing coral reef like this one. This powerful earthquake was followed by a destructive tsunami.

Clues in the Rocks

The earliest evidence of tsunamis comes from the study of Earth's rocks and soil. For example, craters on the seabed indicate that a meteorite or other rock from space might have caused a tsunami. Another sign of a tsunami is a layer of material from the seafloor in rocks far inland.

ACROSS THE PACIFIC

Geologists know that an earthquake long ago caused the coast of Washington State in to sink by 5 feet (1.5 m). Along the coast they found the remains of trees that had been killed as they sank beneath the sea. By studying **tree growth rings**, scientists knew that the most recent ring had formed in 1699, so the earthquake must have occurred in late 1699 or early 1700. To see if this quake caused a tsunami across the Pacific Ocean, scientists checked Japanese written records. They discovered that a 11.5-foot (3.5-m) high tsunami struck villages in eastern Japan on January 27, 1700. By analyzing these Japanese details, scientists discovered that the quake was far stronger than they had originally thought.

TSUNAMIS IN THE WESTERN PACIFIC

East of mainland Asia, several tectonic plates come into contact with each other. The massive Pacific Plate moves northwestward and comes into contact with the North American Plate and the Australian Plate, which are moving in other directions. The smaller Philippine Plate is also moving northwestward into the Eurasian Plate.

Flores, Indonesia, 1992

In 1992, an earthquake occurred off the coast of the island of Flores in Indonesia. The islanders had little time—only two minutes—after the earthquake to get away from the coast before the tsunami reached the shore. About 2,500 people died.

Okushiri, Japan, 1993

The people of Japan have always lived with the threat of tsunamis. The last severe Japanese tsunami occurred in 1993. Less than five minutes after an earthquake close to the coast, a series of waves—some as high as 100 feet (30 m)—struck the island of Okushiri. Nearly 200 people died as houses broke apart and boats were swept inland.

An earthquake in northern Japan in 2003 created a 10-foot (3-m) high tsunami. In the town of Hiroo this fishing boat was swept up onto the dock.

In Gizo, Solomon Islands, a member of the U.S. Navy Medical Corps talks to an islander about plans to build a rainwater catcher. Restoring drinking water supplies is one of the first priorities after a tsunami.

Solomon Islands, 2007

In 2007, a tsunami struck the Solomon Islands in the southern Pacific Ocean, following an earthquake off the coast of Gizo Island. It killed 52 people and destroyed entire villages, which were located along the beaches. The palm and bamboo homes were destroyed by the waves.

"We ran for our lives, away from the waves. When we looked back, we saw our house being destroyed. Many buildings . . . near the coast are washed away. Everyone has moved to higher ground. . . . We are going to spend the night in the open. . . . We have no water at all. . . . We need food. . . . We are really scared."

Arnold Pidakere on Gizo, Solomon Islands, 2007.

Helping Hands

After the Solomon Islands disaster, medical help was needed because the only hospital on Gizo Island was underwater. Australia sent six medical teams to care for the injured. The doctors also administered medicines to prevent diseases from breaking out among the survivors, who were camping in the hills because their homes on the coast had been destroyed.

"We swam out of the room, neck-deep in water."

INDIAN OCEAN TSUNAMI DECEMBER 26, 2004

On December 26, 2004, a massive earthquake near western Sumatra in Indonesia, in Southeast Asia, triggered the worst tsunami in hundreds of years. The earth movements began 20 miles (30 kilometers) below the seabed and extended for 1,000 miles (1,600 kilometers) northward. Parts of the seafloor rose by several yards, displacing vast quantities of ocean water. This created a series of waves, which moved eastward and westward away from the earthquake line.

Visitors to coastal areas of Sri Lanka described their experiences:

"When the first wave came in . . . it was a very mild wave. Then the sea [drew] back. . . . It was like someone had pulled the plug on the ocean. . . . Then came this massive wall of water. . . . I saw [people] just being flung into the air like confetti, just blown out of the water."
Arjuna Seneviratna, in a hotel on the southwestern coast of Sri Lanka

"The water started coming under the door. Within a few seconds it was touching the window. We very quickly scrambled to get out as the windows started to cave in and glass shattered everywhere. We swam out of the room, neck-deep in water, forcing our way through the tables and chairs in the restaurant and up into a tree."
Roland Buerk, in a beach house on the south coast of Sri Lanka

This is the Sumatran coast and the city of Banda Aceh, six weeks after the tsunami. It is still difficult to see where the sea stops and the land begins.

On the southwestern coast of Sri Lanka, waves derailed this train, which crashed into a house.

Sumatra and Thailand

The tsunami that moved eastward struck parts of Sumatra's coast in about twenty minutes. The city of Banda Aceh was totally destroyed and 150,000 people in Sumatra died. The waves continued to the western coast of Thailand, destroying many coastal vacation resorts and killing about 8,000 people.

Destruction in the West

The tsunami traveling westward reached eastern India and Sri Lanka less than two hours after the earthquake. In these countries more than 40,000 people died. Some waves even reached the coast of eastern Africa several hours later, killing hundreds of people in Somalia.

PREVENTING ANOTHER DISASTER

Immediately after the tsunami, people realized that the Indian Ocean needed an earthquake and tsunami warning system like the one that already existed in the Pacific Ocean. By 2006, only two years after the disaster, a new warning system was operating throughout the Indian Ocean.

" I was shocked to see . . . fishing boats flying on the shoulder of the waves, going back and forth into the sea, as if made of paper . . . fishermen were still holding onto them."

P. Ramanamurthy, in Andra Pradesh, India.

TSUNAMIS IN THE AMERICAS

The entire western coast of the Americas lies along the edges of colliding tectonic plates. Three of the very biggest earthquakes of the twentieth century took place near these coasts.

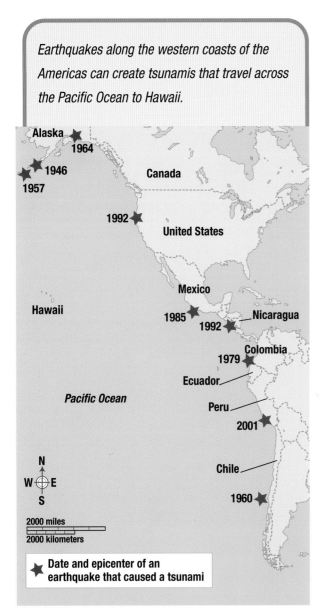

Earthquakes along the western coasts of the Americas can create tsunamis that travel across the Pacific Ocean to Hawaii.

Alaska 1964
1946
1957
Canada
1992
United States
Mexico
Hawaii
1985 Nicaragua
1992
Colombia
1979
Ecuador
Pacific Ocean
Peru
2001
Chile
N
W ⊕ E
S
1960

2000 miles
2000 kilometers

★ Date and epicenter of an earthquake that caused a tsunami

Alaska, 1946

The first of these powerful quakes was near the Aleutian Islands off the coast of Alaska in 1946. On nearby Unimak Island, the waves reached a height of 138 feet (42 m) and completely destroyed a lighthouse, killing its five crew members. The tsunami also raced southward across the Pacific Ocean, reaching the coasts of California and South America. It even produced 33-foot (10-m) high waves in French Polynesia in the southern Pacific Ocean. Hawaii, a

"Along the shore [a great wave] tore up cottages and trees as it swept onward with irresistible force. . . . At the fort a cannon with its carriage, estimated at four tons in weight, was moved 15 feet inward. A schooner [two-masted sailing ship] was left in the midst of the ruins, 200 yards from the beach."

Charles Darwin's description of a tsunami in Concepción, Chile, 1835.

16

A scientist at the Pacific Tsunami Warning Center in Hawaii looks at data from scientific equipment in the Pacific Ocean that might indicate a tsunami.

chain of islands in the central Pacific, suffered the most damage. Five hours after the earthquake, the tsunami killed 159 people in Hawaii and the waterfront area of the town of Hilo was destroyed.

Chile, 1960

In 1960, the most powerful earthquake ever recorded occurred off the coast of Chile in South America. The tsunami that followed soon hit the coast, killing up to 2,000 people. It also traveled across the Pacific Ocean. Once again, Hawaii was in its path. This time 61 people died. The tsunami moved on and reached the coast of Japan, where the waves were still powerful enough to claim 138 more lives.

PROBLEMS FOR HAWAII

More than 50 tsunamis have struck Hawaii in the past 200 years. Five of these were caused by distant earthquakes, which could not be felt in Hawaii. Soon after the 1946 tsunami, the Pacific Tsunami Warning Center was created in Hawaii. It detects earthquakes and ocean waves throughout the Pacific Ocean, and sends out warnings. The people who died in the 1960 tsunami were those who ignored warnings. Now everyone in Hawaii knows they must get away from the sea to higher ground if a warning is broadcast on TV or radio.

"A black wall of water was rapidly building up."

ALASKA MARCH 29, 1964

In the early evening on Good Friday, 1964, the most powerful earthquake ever recorded in North America occurred off the coast of Alaska. It was followed by a tsunami that traveled down the western coast of North America as far as California.

Eyewitnesses in Alaska and California described the tsunami:

"As I circled over the downtown area I observed several large fishing boats floating and crashing into buildings near the boat harbor. **Debris** choked the channel as it hurried out into the bay. With loud booming and snapping, the airways dock and main hanger [were] pulled away from land and sucked out into the rapid current of water in the channel." Bob Leonard, pilot, in Kodiak, Alaska

"In the distance, a black wall of water was rapidly building up.... It was a terrifying mass, stretching up from the ocean floor and looking much higher than the island . . . we both ducked as the water struck, split and swirled over both sides of the island." Peggy Coons, a lighthouse keeper in Crescent City, California

Cities along the West Coast that were affected by the tsunami. The height of the tsunami decreased as it moved south.

Alaska

★ Earthquake epicenter

Valdez 33 ft
Kodiak Island 29.5 ft
Prince William Sound

Canada

Pacific Ocean

Alberni 20 ft — Washington

Coos Bay 13 ft — Oregon
Crescent City 20 ft
Eureka 13 ft

California

San Diego 6.5 ft

| Alberni 20 ft | Place and wave height |

Devastation in the port of Seward, Alaska. Seward suffered a 29.5-foot (9-m) high local tsunami after the waterfront area slumped into the sea during the earthquake.

In southern Alaska, where the waves were highest and arrived the soonest, 119 people died. Luckily two or three small waves hit the coast, alerting many people to move inland or uphill before a much more powerful wave struck. The towns of Valdez, Whittier, Seward, and Kodiak were badly damaged and some Native American coastal villages were destroyed.

Moving Down the Coast

Although the waves became smaller as they moved down the coast, they were still 10 or 13 feet (3 or 4 m) high and caused enormous damage. Some Canadian villages were destroyed. In Oregon, the waves surged up river **estuaries** and rose to greater heights.

AMAZING ESCAPE

Moving House

In Seward, Alaska, Doug McCrae realized a tsunami might follow the earthquake so he helped his wife and infant onto the roof of their house. Soon the tsunami surged in. It tore the house off its **foundations** and carried it through the woods. Amazingly, the family avoided being injured or knocked off by tree branches. Their frightening journey came to an end when the house became wedged between trees. The family climbed into their cold, dark, and wet attic. They spent the freezing night wrapped up in roof insulation material to keep them warm.

Taken by Surprise

Crescent City, California, was badly damaged. The people there experienced three small waves and thought there was little to worry about. The fourth wave— 20 feet (6 m) high—took them by surprise and ten people lost their lives.

LANDSLIDES, GLACIERS, AND VOLCANOES

Not all the waves in the 1964 Alaska tsunami were caused directly by earthquakes. In the Alaskan towns of Valdez and Seward, the quake made the soil behave like liquid, so land and buildings on the waterfronts slumped into the sea. These landslides displaced the water, creating tsunamis up to 33 feet (10 m) high.

Lituya Bay, Alaska

Although displacement of water from above, such as during a landslide, can create large waves locally, they do not seem to travel far. In Lituya Bay, Alaska, in 1958, an earthquake loosened a huge amount of rock at the back of the bay and disturbed a **glacier**. The rocks and ice

"The glacier . . . was jumping and shaking like crazy. Big chunks of ice were falling off the face of it and down into the water . . . then suddenly . . . there was a big wall of water going over the point."

Bill Swanson, in a fishing boat near the entrance to Lituya Bay, Alaska, 1958.

Lituya Bay, Alaska, is almost cut off from the sea, so the 1958 tsunami only affected the bay itself.

THE STOREGGA SLIDE

About 8,000 years ago, a massive underwater landslide occurred at the edge of the **continental shelf** off the coast of Norway. This is known as the Storegga Slide. It triggered a tsunami that crossed the North Atlantic Ocean to Scotland. The waves swept sand from the Scottish coast 50 miles (80 km) inland. Scientists now believe that any underwater landslide that displaces large quantities of material very quickly will trigger a tsunami.

fell nearly 3,280 feet (1,000 m) down the steep mountainsides into the water of the inlet, creating a massive tsunami. The tsunami knocked down trees that were growing on mountain slopes more than 1,640 feet (500 m) above sea level. Outside the bay, however, there was very little evidence of the waves.

Anak Krakatau volcano has formed from what remained of Krakatoa. The volcano is on the Indonesian coast, so an eruption could cause a landslide that would tumble into the ocean and cause a tsunami.

Krakatoa

Tsunamis can also result from volcanic eruptions. In 1883 Krakatoa volcano in Indonesia erupted violently. Hot gases, ash, and rocks swept down the sides of the volcano into the sea. The gases and lighter materials stayed above the surface in a boiling-hot cloud. The larger rocks and stones slid into the water, creating a tsunami that submerged many small islands and destroyed hundreds of coastal villages.

"It reached the tops of the coconut trees."

SAMOA SEPTEMBER 29, 2009

People on affected islands talked about their experiences:

"I saw the tidal wave coming. It was so high it reached the tops of the coconut trees. When it came it ate up the houses. There were people dying on the road and drowning on the beach."
Vavau Moamoa, Samoa

"Our fire services gave out a warning about 10 minutes after the initial earthquake. The emergency services kicked in, all the church bells started ringing in the village, and the good thing is that we've had tsunami drills in the past so we basically knew exactly where to go and the designated areas where we had to go to in the hills."
Olga Keil, Samoa

In the early morning of September 29, 2009, an earthquake began 19 miles (30 km) under the Pacific Ocean on the boundaries of the Pacific and Australian tectonic plates. The movement displaced the seafloor, creating a series of tsunami waves that struck the island shores of Samoa, American Samoa, and Tonga.

Close to the Quake

The islands were so near to the quake's epicenter that there was little time to issue warnings. The tsunami struck the nearest coasts only ten minutes after the quake.

A family in American Samoa outside the wreckage of their tsunami-devastated home.

Three powerful waves—up to 46 feet (14 m) high—destroyed the wooden buildings in coastal villages as they swept hundreds of miles inland. As the waves receded they carried cars and debris out to sea. Worst hit were the villages and vacation resorts along the south coast of Upolu, an island in Samoa.

Abandoned Homes

In Apia, the capital of Samoa, people were warned of the danger and they immediately ran to higher ground. Pago Pago, the capital of American Samoa, was flooded and cars were overturned by the force of the waves.

The tsunami left 226 people dead and thousands homeless. Many of the homeless were too frightened to go back to the coast. Although their families had lived by the sea for centuries they had never experienced such a destructive tsunami before.

Police and rescue workers search for missing people in Lalomanu, Samoa, a week after the tsunami.

Helping Hands

The U.S. government immediately sent a navy ship, two air force planes, and ninety members of the Hawaii National Guard to assist the people of American Samoa. The New Zealand government was equally quick to help Samoa. It immediately sent a plane to search for missing people. This was followed by several large planes carrying medical staff, food, and tents for the homeless. New Zealand helicopters then distributed the supplies around the islands.

PREDICTING TSUNAMIS

The Pacific Tsunami Warning System, based in Hawaii, has been in operation since 1949. Seismometers—machines that measure earth movements—are used throughout the Pacific to detect earthquakes. For sixty years, this system has been very successful in warning about possible tsunamis. Until recently, about 75 percent of the warnings were false alarms, which meant that a lot of money was wasted in preparing for emergencies unnecessarily.

Weighing Water

Since 2002, however, new equipment has made predictions more accurate. Now there are sensors on the Pacific Ocean floor that record the weight of the water. When a tsunami passes over the sensors, they measure the extra weight. The information is sent up to a **buoy** on the

"Tsunamis can travel as fast as jet planes, so rapid assessment following quakes is vital."

Ichiro Fukumori, **oceanographer**.

surface and then by **satellite** to land. Measurements from several sensors in different places show how big a tsunami is and how fast it is moving.

Mapping the Seafloor

Today satellites in space can send down radio signals to measure seafloor movements

Scientists at the Pacific Tsunami Warning Center in Hawaii exchange and pass on information after the September 2009 tsunami in Samoa.

after an earthquake. The information about these changes is fed into a computer, which analyzes the earthquake pattern and predicts the sort of tsunami that may be caused by the movement.

These buoys on a U.S. weather service ship are about to be put in the ocean. They are part of the Pacific Tsunami Warning System and will receive information from sensors on the seafloor.

ANIMAL INSTINCTS

In the hours and minutes just before the 2004 Indian Ocean tsunami, people noticed several species of animals behaving strangely. In a wildlife **sanctuary** in India, flamingos living in low-lying areas flew away to higher ground. In Sri Lanka, elephants at another wildlife park ran away from the beaches an hour before the tsunami arrived. Working elephants in Thailand even broke free from their chains to get away from the coast. Scientists still do not know what the animals are sensing. It may be vibrations in land or air, or changes in Earth's magnetic field. It might simply be that other animals smell and hear an approaching tsunami better than people do.

MINIMIZING THE DAMAGE

In countries where tsunamis are a constant threat, people have taken action to reduce the damage. The Japanese have a very efficient tsunami detection and warning system. They believe they can predict the height, speed, direction, and arrival time of a tsunami anywhere along their shores. They also aim to issue tsunami warnings within two minutes of an earthquake. The message goes to all TV and radio channels and the emergency services.

Lessons from Okushiri

In 1993 on the Japanese island of Okushiri, 198 people died in a tsunami. Now the island is protected by sea walls, as well as by river floodgates, which close automatically after a large earthquake.

> " People in the Pacific region are often taught about [tsunamis] and know when one is about to strike. On beaches in California, Japan and Chile, there are notices warning people to head inland if an earth tremor begins or if the sea starts to recede."
>
> *Marine geologist David Long.*

This floodgate in Numazu, Japan, can drop down to protect the city less than five minutes after an earthquake is detected.

This man in Tamil Nadu, India, owes his life to the young forest of 80,000 trees that villagers planted in 2002. In December 2004, these trees protected the village from the massive Indian Ocean tsunami.

Everyone on the island also has a radio receiver to pick up warnings from a special disaster radio channel. If people are advised to leave their homes they can choose from forty signposted routes into the hills. In addition, in the port of Aonae, a 21.7-foot (6.6-m) high platform has been built to hold 440 people.

Ready for a Tsunami

The Pacific Northwest coast of the United States is another area at high risk from tsunamis. In this region, beaches are equipped with tsunami warning sirens. Each local government has its own emergency plans. In schools, children practice what to do if a tsunami strikes.

MANGROVE FORESTS

After the 2004 Indian Ocean tsunami, scientists discovered that areas of India with coastal **mangrove** forests suffered much less damage than those that were open to the ocean. Villages next to the ocean were destroyed, while nearby villages with a coastal barrier of mangroves were untouched. The mangroves reduced the energy of the tsunami waves. Unfortunately, about a quarter of the mangrove forests in Thailand, India, Sri Lanka, and Indonesia were cut down in the late twentieth century. Many people living around the Indian Ocean now want to replant mangroves for their future protection.

KEEPING SAFE

If you are at risk from tsunamis there are some basic safety rules to remember. If you are on a low-lying coast and you feel an earthquake, you should head for higher ground. If you are on the coast and see the ocean draw back you should immediately run away from the sea—uphill if possible.

Leave the Car Behind

It is often best to avoid using a car because everyone else may do the same and the roads could become blocked. Sometimes roads are cracked or covered by landslides after an earthquake, too.

"If you feel an earthquake, if you see the water retreating, or if you hear a loud roar from the ocean . . . head inland fast. Every step you go inland, even if it's not up, is a step toward safety."

Eddie Bernard, director of the Pacific Marine Environmental Laboratory in Seattle, Washington.

Signs like this one are placed near beaches to remind people to be alert to the dangers of tsunamis.

ENTERING

TSUNAMI
HAZARD ZONE

Coastal residents in Sri Lanka flee from their homes after a tsunami warning. In 2004, 30,000 Sri Lankans died in the Indian Ocean tsunami.

What Not To Do

It is just as important to know what not to do during a tsunami. Never go onto a beach to watch a tsunami because once you see it coming you will not have time to escape. If you have avoided one wave do not return to your home. A tsunami is a series of waves, sometimes over about twelve hours. Often the first wave is not the biggest, so do not think that later waves will be smaller.

Patience Saves Lives

Listen to a radio for the latest information. Never go back to your home until experts tell you it is safe. Tsunamis are far too dangerous for you to take any chances.

AMAZING ESCAPE

Safety in the Trees

After the 1960 earthquake in Chile, many people in the town of Quenuir got into their boats and headed out to sea. They were trying to escape the earthquake, but instead they were caught by the tsunami's first wave and drowned. Other people climbed trees, but many of them died when the force of the waves knocked the trees over. A few people were luckier. One of these was Estalino Hernández. He climbed to the top of a tree and clung on tightly throughout the night as the waves rose up to his waist.

GLOSSARY

buoy A floating object attached to the seafloor.

continental shelf An underwater area next to a continent, which eventually slopes down to the deeper seafloor.

crust The outermost solid layer of Earth, between 3 and 30 miles (5 and 50 km) thick.

debris The remains of broken or destroyed objects.

displace To move out of position.

earthquake A movement of the rocks in Earth's crust.

estuary The part of a river where it meets tidal water from the sea.

foundations The parts of a building under the ground that support the structure above.

geologists Scientists who study Earth's rocks.

glacier A slow-moving mass of ice that is formed from layers of crushed snow.

landslides Fast-moving masses of rocks and debris that rush down a slope.

mangrove A tree that grows in coastal waters in tropical regions.

mantle The 1,900-mile (3,000-km) thick, mainly solid layer of Earth beneath the crust and above the core.

meteorites Debris or rocks from outer space that gets through Earth's atmosphere without being destroyed.

oceanographer A scientist who studies the oceans and the living things in them.

sanctuary A place where wildlife is protected.

satellite An object in orbit around Earth.

tectonic plates The large sections of Earth's crust and upper mantle that move around independently, causing earthquakes.

tree growth rings The circles in a tree trunk, each of which indicates one year's growth.

tremor A shaking of the ground.

whirlpool An area of water moving in a circle and drawing objects down into its center.

FURTHER INFORMATION

Books

Fradin, Judy and Dennis. *Tsunamis*. Witness to Disaster. Des Moines, IA: National Geographic, 2008.

Levy, Janey. *World's Worst Tsunamis*. Deadly Disasters. New York: Rosen, 2009.

Stiefel, Chana. *Tsunamis*. A True Book. New York: Children's Press, 2009.

Townsend, John. *The Asian Tsunami 2004*. When Disaster Struck. Chicago: Heinemann, 2007.

Woods, Michael and Mary B. *Tsunamis*. Disasters Up Close. Minneapolis, MN: Lerner, 2007.

Websites

www.fema.gov/kids/tsunami.htm
The Federal Emergency Management Agency (FEMA) dedicates part of its kids' site to tsunamis.

www.pbs.org/wgbh/nova/tsunami/
This interactive website features maps, diagrams, and animation of tsunamis, as well as answers to common questions. There is also a link to watch the PBS show on the 2004 Indian Ocean tsunami.

http://pubs.usgs.gov/circ/c1187
A site designed by the U.S. Geological Survey that has interviews with survivors of the 1960 Chile tsunami, as well as advice about how best to survive a tsunami.

www.tsunami.noaa.gov/
The National Oceanic and Atmospheric Administration (NOAA) maintains a website with information on what a tsunami is, how a tsunami forms, and how to stay safe in the event of a tsunami.

INDEX

Page numbers in **bold** are photographs or diagrams